So Many Unsaid Things

So Many Unsaid Things
Edited & Compiled by Vandana Sudheesh
Print Edition

First Published in India in 2021
Inkfeathers Publishing
New Delhi 110095

ISBN 978-93-90882-27-4

www.inkfeathers.com

So Many Unsaid Things

Edited & Compiled by

Vandana Sudheesh

Inkfeathers Publishing

Disclaimer

The anthology "So Many Unsaid Things" is a collection of 72 Poems written by 36 authors who belong to different parts of the globe.

The anthology editor and the publisher have ensured to make the content as reader-friendly and plagiarism-free as possible. Unless otherwise indicated, all the names, characters, objects, businesses, places, events, incidents- whether physical/non-physical, real/unreal, tangible/ intangible in whatsoever description used in this book are either the product of the author's imagination or used in a fictitious manner.

The poems published in this book are solely owned by their respective authors and are in no way intended to hurt anyone's religious, political, spiritual, brand, personal or fanatic beliefs and/or faith, whatsoever.

In case, any sort of plagiarism is detected in the poems within this anthology or in case of any complaints or grievances or objections, neither the anthology editor nor the publisher is to be held responsible.

Co-Authored By

Aastha Khera | Abhav Gupta | Ananya Mishra

Ananya Purba Sengupta | C.L. Williams | Divya Naveen

Gunjan Makhijani | Hrishikesh Mokashi | Jagruthi Kommuri

Jeysanaah Ganesh | Kriti | Madhurya Kommuri | Manoj Vaz

Miriam Benjamin | Munmun Aidasani | Prajwal Shukla

Prasann Sharma | Rachna Goyal | Rajalakshmi Kurup

Ramaponni P | Shreesh Swaraj | Siddhi Menon | Siya Kohli

Sneha Sabu | Soumya Tewari | Sreeja Chaudhuri | Sreekala Ajay

Sujatha Menon | Swathi Umashankar | Swati Pillai

Tanushree Keshan | Vaishnavi Rajput | Vedika Pathania

Vishakha Naware | Vandana Sudheesh | Anush Goel

Contents

Meet The Editor

Vandana Sudheesh

Vandana Sudheesh, a poet with a diverse voice, was born in Kozhikode district in the southern Indian state of Kerala. She was conferred with the WORLD AWARD "CESAR VALLEJO 2020" for EXCELLENCE IN LITERARY FIELD by UHE (Union Hispanomundial De Escritores) in Spanish. Also, she was awarded the WORLD PRIZE POETRY AWARD (1st place from ASIAN CONTINENT) for a posthumous tribute to the great poet Kairat

Duessinov Parman, founding President of WNWU (World Nations Writers Union). Also, she was conferred with the Order of Shakespeare Medal in 2021. She is a moderator of Motivational Strips and directs Asian writers through a parliamentary committee of forum members. Considering her passion, enthusiasm, and contribution to world literature, she was awarded the membership of the World Nation Writers Union (WNWU). She published her first solo book "The Humble Wrath" in August 2020. She started writing under the influence of world-famous writers from an early age. After completing her MBA, she worked for Axis Bank Limited in India and later went to Early Retirement. She then devoted herself to composing poetry. To date, her poems have been written in four collections of poetry named Poets Unify World, A Gift-III. She is also a regular contributor to Indian newspapers and magazines. She is also a regular contributor to Web Magazine and Social Media. Notable among these is Dhoni and Irreplaceable Legend, Aroma of Notion by Oxigle Press, Bharat Vision by Motivational Strips. Apart from writing, she is also a dancer, an artist and a singer.

Editor's Note

At times there is a space called silence when things go unsaid in each of our lives. Would we slip away from reality? Would we be sipping coffee with tunes of desires that we wished have happened?

We might have lost any ray of hope. It is never created but formed out of either emerging emotions that once hurt us or kept as a secret. Every time I had a question as to how we can fill the empty bottle of silence. I wish I could wet the paper with those emotions which are left unsaid. Words have the power within to unleash the dark.

Why don't we write it down and let it go out of our suffocation shelves? We can find a little happiness to grow every day. We all are surrounded by many memories unsaid or unseen which we wanted to tell someone and release the burden of our hearts. Those thoughts get piled up like old books which will never be opened again.

Spilling them unto the paper makes us free of that terrible feeling and it helps to build a castle of satisfaction from inside. You must carry them no more with you into the grave.

This thought is the reason I have compiled this book "SO MANY UNSAID THINGS." There are unique feelings that are shared, which you can read in this book with too many unsolved questions finally solved. I wish after every read you have so much to think about and it becomes relatable. A splendid read resonating the inner voices of the readers' minds. With all my soul I wish you all a happy reading with much love.

Happy journey,

Vandana Sudheesh

So Many Unsaid Things

My Doubtful Heart

by Vandana Sudheesh

My mind stronger than your words,
Always tried to render rendezvous with succour.
You stole my heart for no reason,
Where are you gone now with your inner desire?
Many things unsaid just burnt within my eyes,
Suffocation penetrates the rumble of my heart,
Turned me upside down to relocate the existence of my soul.
I ran and got stuck in the doubtful field of love.
I can hardly breathe to utter your name ethereally,
I was lost in the middle of the desert where I choked on your images.

Seven

by Manoj Vaz

Trapped with nowhere to turn,
Life changing beyond my control.
Ego to pacify, money to burn,
A ruthless pride rules my soul.

Hungry but not to nourish,
Baying for flesh and blood.
Always starting but never to finish,
An insatiable chasm, greed, my food.

Rage, the other side of resentment,
Filled with despair, brimming doubt.
The excruciating distress doesn't relent,
Wrath is with what my mind is fraught.

Cringing, crying, not able to express,
Nothing but malice oozing from my core.
The feeling of comparative worthlessness,
Alas! Envy brings my frailty to the fore.
When carnal becomes the cardinal,

With silent screams none can hear.
The morals bowing low to the physical,
It is lust, the rape of my mind, I fear.

I try to speak but my mouth is full,
Living to eat not eating to live.
Not the storm but definitely the lull,
Gluttony is recrement that deprive.
Indolence walks with me thru' the day,
And sleeps with me unblinking at night.
Unable to break chains, I quietly lay,
Sloth leaves me depleted, no will to fight.

The seven sins make me human bound,
Life, time, wasted and badly spent.
With no courage to turn things around,
A deluge of hurt, a torrent of repent.

Keeping me anchored to this remorse,
The seven reigns despite me crying foul.
Yet, looking within me, I converse,
Solace, please pacify and calm my soul.

Twinkle Twinkle

by Manoj Vaz

The bright flashes followed her soul,
She posed but the anguish strode on,
The world shone but her mind ran foul,
Like swarming wasps in a race bygone.

No matter how her tears were shed,
In the confines of her velvety bed,
No matter how hard she screamed,
They were trapped inside her head.

As she sold herself at the human mart,
The sea became her embodied quilt,
Waves crashing heavily in her heart,
Drowning her conscience in a sea of guilt.

The weight of perfection scaled her gain,
Her eyes betrayed the contrived smile,
Her soft lips cracked by a lifetime of pain,
While retching and tasting human bile.
The sea lured her as it had always done,

The waves serenaded her as fate frowned,
The battle of stardom she had won,
But her breath in the abyss, drowned.

Where There Is No Will

by Manoj Vaz

I have the will to do something,
But no will to know what.
Because I will fall for anything,
At the drop of a metaphorical hat.
I have a lot to accomplish,
And a lot of time to not spend.
After all, you can't vilify a fish,
For not swimming on land.
Potential is for the achievers,
Don't hate or vilify me,
For not being like the others,
My thoughts are for me, let me be.

Dust to dust, ashes to ashes,
What is it you gain in the rat race?
A body full of pain and aches,
And prove a better rat, just in case.

Life may have dealt me a great hand,
Remember, I am the joker in the pack.
Whatever jackpot I may land,
It won't give me my time back.
Peace of mind is happily priceless,
Income is merely a means to an end,
To get through life without a fuss,
Why drive yourself around the bend?
The sky is blue to the naked vision,
But space is dense and dark with no light,
So, don't get fooled by the illusion,
And lose your beauty sleep at night.
One day you will die and be forgotten,
Your struggles, your potential, dead to all.
When your soul is ready to pass the baton,
You will be happy you had no will.

Poli-Chess (n)

by Manoj Vaz

"The deadly strategy game
where pawns are sacrificed
so that the King may win."

The coveted land, 64 squares in the fray,
Some painted white, all morbidly black.
The players who control are always grey,
With the common pawns taking the flak.

The drama queens rule this motley roost,
Making promises with no intention to keep.
What can the common pawn do at the most,
Memories too short, five long years to reap.

Riots, rapes, murders, and corruption galore,
Knights, bishops, rooks dancing to a tune.
Despondency creeps, it has happened before,
Only symbols change, the disease, immune.

Towards destruction they bravely advance,
Following orders while the kings, retreat.
The despotic band is on, pawns must dance,
Though their children have nothing to eat.

Oddly though, it is the pawns that vote,
And it's not that the pawns are mad,
They know in electoral triumph and defeat,
Politicians come only in bad and less bad.

Unlock

by Manoj Vaz

As we slip through the cracks of time damned,
Caged, cursed, incarcerated like beasts of yore.
Nothing glows more than the soul awakened,
An unlocking, that has never happened before.

Governments will come as they will go,
The blame game won't help the stricken world.
Race and colour don't matter, all lives do,
Humans discriminate, viruses just get unfurled.

The existential truth we so ardently search,
That screams it's too short a day to be selfish.
Lies beyond the wall, we are afraid to breach
While we wait for our numbers to diminish.

Who said that the promised journey will be easy?
Who said you won't have to run that extra mile?
Innocents will perish for the sins of supremacy,
But in the end, the arrival must be worthwhile.

What do you risk but your insignificance?
Why can't we change, forgive and mend?
The time you feel everything is decadence,
That time will be the beginning, my friend.

Life On A String

by Manoj Vaz

Intrepid by nature, the kite was exhilarated,
The gusty winds, the gutsy irreverence set upon.
The pain in his heart purposefully berated,
Soar as he may, it was a battle not to be won.

The sky clouded grey but his heart blue,
The grounds longing, trees bracing for a fight,
The strings that held his heart had no clue,
It now dangled from a malignant kite.

What was unshackled had turned servient,
As he released the kite in an ascending soar.
The reel of serendipity hung on the deviant,
The rain set to strangle evert breath of air.

His heart, flimsy, frail, forever in pain,
A slave to the strings forever attached,
Tangled, knotted, bleeding in the rain,
Hungry to breathe, thirsty to live detached.

As the sun broke the dark clouds' reign,
He looked all over, his kite couldn't be found
'Cos caught by the winds, torn by the rain
His mangled heart had spiralled to the ground.

The End of Time

by Manoj Vaz

Explicitly, essentially, eventually; eternity will end,
The world as we know it will cease to exist.
The sun rising won't bring newfound ways to mend,
Spirits won't rejuvenate even for the optimist.

Distant stars may twinkle, celestial planets, shine,
If we think ourselves to be the centre of creation,
The rancidity of our flesh and toxicity of our bones,
Will find lament in our karmic soul definition.

Frozen, stuck in time, residing in a loveless abyss,
Dead souls breathing cosmic oxygen meant for life.
The trance takes over the rhythm of beating hearts,
Being able to stand in the universe will be strife.

Lilies, orchids and roses arranged in a floral sphere,
Alas my departed, it is a wreath, not a bouquet.
An iridescent barrage of aromatic fragrances here,
This is where my broken heart finds a tourniquet.

I press my skull against the veneered coffin walls,
Tortured in darkness as chaos consumes my soul.
Ambushed from devilish corners of unknown calls,
Forgive me universe, for I know I have done foul.

The Crippled Puppy

by Manoj Vaz

The boy from the slum on the railway route,
Yearned for a companion, a pet, so bad.
He shone shoes with a brush and soot,
Collecting pennies to visit the pet store ahead.

A friend to hug close on wintery nights,
A friendly bark, a vigorous wag, a moist lick,
Shivering through the dark to morning light,
Alone in a sea of humans with skins so thick.

The pet shop was wagging with bonnie puppies,
Different breeds, some pedigree others not.
Yet none to be sold for his hard-earned pennies,
Till he came across a limping, bleary eyed tot.

Take him for free, the shop keeper said,
But the boy knew the puppy's worth.
He emptied his pocket at the counter stand,
Promising five coins a week for twelve weeks forth.

The man's curiosity filled his mind like ants,
Why a crippled dog, he tried to judge.
The boy then pulled up his ill-fitting pants,
To show he had a wooden stump for a leg.

The Loudness of Everything Left Unsaid

(Thoughts That Kill Us Everyday)

by Munmun Aidasani

So much of what we live goes on inside,
Is always more than what we dare confide.
The bitterest tears shed over graves,
For the words which left unsaid.

It is the love never confessed, and words left unspoken,
Not everyone can heal the broken.
A sorry left too late, even knowing,
Anyone's life could not wait.

The unsaid truth, the last good-bye,
When your heart aches for the ones whom you loved, die.
It is the forgiveness never given,
For the bitter moments, to the ones who are already in heaven.

It is the unsaid feeling, the whisper of words in the head,
When a daughter bid-adieu her dad's home and
begin a new life ahead.
It is the desires remain unfulfilled,
When all your dreams which you discovered got killed.

It is the sadness or depression, when you were unheard,
No one bothered how you felt and what you preferred.
It is the diaries of grief, the tongue-tied aches,
Everything shatters, everything breaks.

But it is never too late, you are alive,
you still have a chance to speak,
Words that could help to save a life
or give strength to someone weak.
A few things spilling out of mind,
is not always better to left unsaid,
Because all that will ever remain is the silence, lying dead.

Feelings Unsaid...Remembrance

by Munmun Aidasani

The flowers representing remembrance, when life is done,
A bunch of red poppies as tribute to the loved ones,
Who have gone before us, the race they have won.
Life is a resting place along the road, to reach sweet eternity,
To find some true reality, in beautiful infinity.

A new berth waits you on the other side,
The past and present unite there, beneath time's flowing tide.
For some the journey is quicker,
For some the journey is slow,
Far greater than we know.

So thy thoughts, when thou are gone,
Love itself shall slumber on.
In the shadow of my sorrow, past the whisper of goodbye,
How to wipe tears away, when eyes are dry?
A thousand words sunk in with my soul left unsaid,
Even when I tried to use those words in a hundred ways, I failed.

Thoughts were spinning in my head,
I wish, if you could hear instead,
But emotions are still there until they fade.

The one who are out of sight,
Would remain immortal in memory throughout my life.
All I have the tormented memories as treasures, and picture in a frame,
All the precious moments, ever still the same.

Be Mine?

by Swati Pillai

We will write our story in the sands of time,
When enough waves have washed the shores,
When enough rain has washed the Earth,
When enough people have forgotten about us,
When enough life has been washed away.

We will reminisce the days of when we found true love,
How days and nights, darkness and light,
All turned into one...
How a minute in waiting seemed like a year,
Hours together seemed a blur.

How a gentle caress or the touch of your hands
Would make my heart skip a beat.
When my happiness was yours, and your tears, mine.
When life has washed away enough time...

Be Mine?

I Am Tired

by Madhurya Kommuri

Strongest warriors have the toughest battles they say trying to give some comfort,
But what if that badge of honour does not outshine the hurt?

What if I am tired to take this any forward,
What if I have more than enough suffered,
And can no longer hold on to my record?

What if I am done keeping my voice covered,
What if my future does seem to be a desert,
And had enough lessons from life learnt?

What if so much injustices life did offer,
What if things are all blur and unclear,
And I can no longer handle it like a master?

What if I am tired of always being alert,
What if those words seem to me absurd,
And no longer as a warrior I wish to be referred?

What if I am tired to keep my mind in divert,
What if to a vulnerable child I wish to revert,
And to be that strong warrior I no more covet?

What if life's truth I have already uncovered,
But from the wounds I will never be recovered?
I know I sound like a lost coward,
With spirit and head lowered
But what if I really am exhausted and tired?

Not Everything You Lose is A Loss

by Madhurya Kommuri

I lost you from my heart,
You lost me from your life.
I don't know about your life, but my heart is peaceful now.

I lost your name from my prayers,
You lost my name from your blessing.
I don't know how cursed you got, but my prayers are answered now.

I lost someone who kept me hanging,
You lost someone who could have given you everything.
I don't know how is everything with you now, but there is no one who would even hang up on me.

I lost someone who couldn't even choose me,
You lost someone who gave you all the priority.
I don't know if anyone would choose you now, but I wouldn't even be treated as a choice.

I don't know what you wish for me now, vengeance or guilt.
But I only hope for you to be able to love someone like I did
and to get the same back unlike I didn't.

Promises You Couldn't Keep

by Madhurya Kommuri

Promises you couldn't keep;
Is it because I was not worth it
Or is my love for you too deep?

Promises you couldn't keep;
Everything you ever said and did,
Like demons inside my head they creep.

Promises you couldn't keep;
Every night they haunt me
And disturb my sleep.

Promises you couldn't keep;
I wish I didn't let you inside
And hadn't taken that leap.

Promises you couldn't keep;
I could do nothing but weep.
Darling now I just want to tell you this
that "what you sow is what you reap."

You Don't Know

by Madhurya Kommuri

I know this will make you laugh,
How I wanted you to be my better half.

You don't know how hard I love,
You don't know how bad you hurt.

You don't know and I can hardly say,
That so badly I want you to stay.

I don't know how easily you hide,
That together we smiled.

I don't know how you could lie,
And that made me cry.

You don't know how hard I tried,
For you a million miles I would ride.
Yet you denied.

Is Someone There?

by Madhurya Kommuri

My hands sweat,
My heart aches,
My body it shakes.
But is someone there
Who even cares?

Sometimes my eyes rain,
Succumbing to this pain.
To the demons in my mind I'm chained.
But is someone there
Who even cares?

I pull myself near,
Trembling with fear.
My silent cries which no body hear.
But is someone there
Who even cares?

What about the times when it's
Not my eyes but my heart that bleeds,
Into depths of trauma it leads,
And I'm left quite indeed.

But is someone there
Who even cares?
My room doors I close,
Laying numb on the floor,
Crying more and more.
But is someone there
Who even cares?

This agony it kills,
I gulp many pills,
Oh God! Like hell it feels.
But is someone there
Who even cares?

There are wounds so deep,
Which I myself am afraid to peep,
And this to myself I keep.
But is someone there
Who even cares?

On papers, walls I scribble,
Wanting myself to strangle,
With pain I struggle,
Life or death-what to choose,
Fed up and my control I lose.
But is someone there
Who even cares?

My strength as a prey to the sorrow it bends,
To kill myself my heart tends.
Only if there's someone to befriend
whose ears they could lend,
My wounds would definitely mend.
But is someone there
Who even cares?

Is someone there
Who really cares?
Someone when I dial,
To stay a little while,
Walk the extra mile,
To bring back my smile?

What is Love?

by Madhurya Kommuri

Is it as simple as my heart when it found you? Or as complicated as my mind when it thinks of losing you?

Is it when my heart skipped a beat when I saw you for the first time?
Or is it when I fell for you deeper walking by your side?

Is it when people say, "Have you lost your mind?" Seeing me daydreaming about you?
Or is it when I found my true courageous self-fighting for you?

Is it when your look took my breath away?
Or is it when your touch breathes
life into my broken pieces?

Is it a mystery as deep as your eyes?
Or is it the answer I found in your smile?

Is it when my quest ended when you held my hand? Or is it how my pursuit to hold it forever began?

Tree of Death

by Shreesh Swaraj

Surrounded by dark,
Hollowed by lull,
Thoughtless where to start,
Stood I, facing the Tree of Death.

Looking somewhere to hide,
Shivering from deep inside,
Was this the end, I thought,
Stood I, facing the Tree of Death.

Deadly zephyr hustling with leaves,
Howling its glory, leaving me bleak!
Killing inside me hopes of being freed,
Stood I, facing the Tree of Death.

Do you think I didn't try?
Ran I, down the never-ending aisle,
Hope to find someone besides,
Only to find nothing's worthwhile.

Knelt I pleading Death for mercy,
Forgive me for the sins I carry.
Oblivion is a state of peace,
Said the merciless, not to worry.

For the last, I looked at my past.
How beautiful this journey been,
Realized I, seeking my inner peace.
Smiling profusely, stood I bold,
Eyes closed, leaving my soul.
Leaving the merciful Tree of Death,
Saw I, the mystic aura it held.

The Sound of Silence

by Jagruthi Kommuri

The loudest shout one can ever hear,
Is the sound of silence, that we all still,
Many are the feelings we hide of fear,
That when we try to express phrases are nil.

The voices that we hear in our head,
Are so loud that they make us muzzle,
And they are well buried before even said,
Yet in the background they always rustle;

But silence is so powerful, it can kill and also heal,
Cause those feelings aren't a lie they're real,
Yes, silence isn't heard cause sometimes it is felt,
Just like words, even with silence true ones will melt.

Mask

by Jagruthi Kommuri

I have my true self just like you do,
But just as you hide it, I hide it too,
We all feel so shy to be true and our own,
Cause though we are kids we think we are grown.

Everyone is searching for someone to be true,
But could find any because no one ever knew,
That though we ever pass by all our ways through.
Never we find that someone cause we all hide from view,
And we all have our 'self' that we hide so well,
One day we wouldn't recognise though our mask fell.

My Thoughts

by Jagruthi Kommuri

Deep are my thoughts instilled,
Ever I yearn, never fulfilled.
Of what would have been,
If I was so keen,
Of who I would be,
If I had been me.

Or why is it tough,
Just to be enough,
Or what do I long,
When to me I belong,
Because,
I'm not just the thoughts I build,
I'm also the thoughts I've killed.

Because

by Jagruthi Kommuri

Because of what's fake, I know what is real,
Because I was hurt before, so now I can heal,
I know what's right now, because I knew what's wrong.

Because I was weak before, now I'm made strong,
Because I was lost before, now I can be found,
I can now swim because before I was drowned;

Because,
I was shy before to be whom I want to be,
I am now what I am, my true self that you see,
Because,
You'll know what it is to have, only if you have lost,
You'll know the value of life, when you know what it will cost.

May Be I

by Jagruthi Kommuri

May be I'm not your best friend,
But I wish if I could be one,
May be I don't know what inspires you,
But mine with you has begun,
May be I'm not who you wanted,
But I'll be the friend you need,
May be I don't know what you love,
But my love for you will never recede,
May be I don't know your fears and doubts
But in you I'll always believe,
May be I can never understand you,
But I promise I'll never ever leave,
May be I don't know why we ever met,
But you are very special of all the rest,
May be all I can do is only wish,
And yet I'll wish you only the best.

See You Again May Be Not

by Jagruthi Kommuri

The next time we meet,
Will be so lovely and sweet,
To see your eyes of magic,
Like stars lonely and tragic.

Only if you could see them as I,
You'd know the reason why,
That every time you pass by,
I'm lost in their beauty and lie.

To have known you all this while,
And to capture your baby smile,
Even if there's distance of miles,
To see you again is all worthwhile.

But as life is always changing its view,
And lovely persons like you are few,
In this life of uncertain chances we get,
What were the odds that we could've met.

So even if you are not here to stay,
I'm blessed to have met you on my way,
For the rest of my life's story,
You'll remain the best memory.

Decisions

by Kriti

I looked again at the message, yet another decision to take
I made the imaginary list, asking which side will win?
To choose yes, we must agree with the no
To choose one, we must let go the other
To choose today, we must rethink about the past and future
All this to avoid the burden of regret.

I scratch my head and toss the list aside
Why is this so difficult? I ask in frustration with life
Does everyone overthink for a simple decision?
It's time to flip that coin and leave things on fate
Well not as easy as said, let's bring back that list
After hours and days of contemplating,
Maybe this time there won't be an "if".

Every moment lived, is a decision to stay
To stay and survive this turn of events
Life, misfortune, or a blessing in disguise?
Time reveals that after we finally decide

But let me tell you something,
Decisions are always tough to take.

Today

by Kriti

Dragging myself like a zombie,
Will today be the same?
Snoozed that never-ending alarm game again,
Looked at the time, 5 more minutes I say
Is it something that can be cancelled I think,

Will have to get up even today
Finding some distractions in phone,
It is now time to avoid thoughts by work
Let one stress be replaced by another
Let the thoughts that disturb vanish for a day

Let's make the to do list for today
The end of the list in the real beginning
That's where the mysteries come back
Finding the purpose of life
Or simply contemplating a decision,

Thinking about the lessons learnt
Or plan for the far ahead,
Maybe today was a fear lived
Or it also could have been an achievement,
Today was all the same and different both.

It's Okay

by Sreeja Chaudhuri

It's okay if you fail.
It's okay if your ship could not sail.
It's okay if they say you are not a beauty
Because pleasing their eyes is not your duty.
It's okay if you think you don't have any talent.
That won't make your life unpleasant.
It's okay if others think you are bad
Don't let their thoughts make you mad.
It's okay if he doesn't love you anymore
A lot of love might be waiting for you in store.
It's okay if you don't have any friends
Because it's better to have no one than the one who only pretends.
It's okay if they laugh
Making others laugh is also a craft.
It's okay to feel unloved
Be your own beloved.
We humans are imperfect
And that's what makes us so perfect

We will all fail,
We will all cry
But our hope for a better day
Should never die.

What I Couldn't Tell You

by Miriam Benjamin

I was lying next to you last night;
one of the more comfortable silences hung over us.
My arms were wrapped in yours,
my toes curled up next to your heels,
my chest could feel your steady breathing
my heart, the growing calmness.
I whispered your name.
You heard of course, and asked me what had happened;
I didn't respond.
For how could I tell you that even though my body gets to feel you, it is not enough?
I need my voice to hold you too.
What I couldn't tell you was that I wanted to chant your name like an incantation,
to let your presence linger on my lips for as long as it could,
to make you understand that eternal longing that's within me when it comes to you,
to show you how full of love I am that the only thing that makes sense to me is your name.

I repeat it in my head,
Over
and over
and over
and over
till it slowly softens.

Let's Think

by Prajwal Shukla

"Let's think", said my father.
As I asked him for an idea,
To scribble some cloth paint on a faded old t-shirt,
As a project in my craft class,
"Let's Think", I said as I made a mess.
By pouring all my heart into coming up with something cool,
"Let's Think!" He said would look great on a t-shirt,
Just the two words: together by themselves,
With creative and supportive ideas,
And with each footstep of my life,

Gathering every single gram of courage,
I tried to live as I thought I deserved to,
But growing up on the hefty side of the scale,
Tilting down the seesaw,
The line between friends and bullies,

Began to blur out of sight,
And for another decade to follow,
This suffocation crowded my mind,
Always in fear, that showing my-self,
Or anything I made, was going to be,

Mocked, trolled, belittled, and sublimed,
I grew up thinking,
"Is this all that I am?"
A laughingstock,
A device for entertainment,

For the very souls, I thought,
Were next in line,
To family of mine,
This led to a rollercoaster of syndromes,
Making me feel like a failure,
A loser of some kind,

No matter what my achievements,
A mere fraud I saw them see me,
This crisis was of my identity,
And my existence,
Because for when my presence was...
Unfathomably destroyed.

It was hard, too hard,
And unthinkable for my body,
Or my mind or even my soul,
To seek out in hope,
That one day it's will,
It will find.
But taking therapeutic actions
Leading a struggle to prove myself.
I understand that there's no care,
No way, no remorse,
For my reason to be there,

It wasn't going to be me,
Or my anything
That would or could affect their minds,
But me, myself and I...
That should be the only important one,

That I choose to satisfy.
For the way of my will,
Will they never see.
And seeking me out,
Is my journey.

So I lay myself open to those,
And take a deep breath,
To finish the sentence I once left unsaid,
For hence forth the t-shirt shall read,
"Let's think before we speak."

Until We Meet Again in Another Life

by Hrishikesh Mokashi

Betrayal is a ten letter word
Usually practiced by a coward.
Lessons in life are learnt the hard way,
To be spared the pain, is all that u pray.
Promises made, seldom are kept.
Love, respect, ardour in the blink of an eye, swept.
The best love songs speak of numbing sorrow,
Strawberries and champagne earmarked for another tomorrow.
The soulful voice, resonating with passion,
Arousing unwanted feelings of love and adoration
Stirring the reluctant embers of long lost emotion
To what purpose is such immortal admiration?
An anachronism of sorts, inexplicable,
Of undying devotion to duty most capable.
Inflicting immense grief inadvertently
Or on purpose - gleefully?
Lingering glances speak without saying,
Of the turmoil and heartache with which you are paying
For the folly of unrequited feeling.

Only a look and a voice remain - fleeting,
With never a chance of ever again meeting.
Darkness and silence, resounding, reverberating,
With the crushed hope and loss devastating.
Why? A question to remain forever unanswered,
Emotions and tears flowing free, completely unfettered.
Thy purpose lord, one cannot see,
Perhaps it was never meant to be.
Our paths should never have crossed at all,
Habits changed, a life forever transformed by your call,
The haunting memories of books and songs shared,
Only to you beloved, my soul I barred.
Alas! If only you knew how much I cared.
Ships that pass each other in the night,
Is that what destiny proclaimed should be our plight?
Perpetual sadness after a petty fight,
A deep dark void - Fate laughs with all her might!
It requires courage to fight all odds,
Sometimes one needs to even challenge the gods.
Time - the great healer will play its part,
In this lifetime, may fade the memories of the heart.
But in the next, will rekindle the connection,
Because ours is an eternal affection.
Time itself must then accept defeat,
When at last, two yearning hearts and souls, reunite and replete.

Living The Dream

by Hrishikesh Mokashi

Dreams and aspirations it is,
Something that everyone's got;
Well, it is our ultimate goal
And it has to be sought.

And let me tell you guys, that it isn't that hard
If you have got an ounce of hope
You will break all the barriers
With all the obstacles you cope...

However bad the situation is,
In yourself you have got to believe
The difficulties just dissolve off
And then nothing is hard to achieve.

Be it a hindrance or be it a pain
Through it all you've got to endure,
It's all a little illness that
Endurance can surely cure...

But just all this is futile,
'Cause determined you've got to be-
All bars will step aside
For determination is the key!

Have faith in your failures
As towards success they lead your way,
Don't be afraid of them because
They've got to go away...

So this is the life mantra, my friends!
However hard it seems:
Never ever give up, I repeat.
Living up your dreams

The March

by Hrishikesh Mokashi

The leaf rustles on a lonely tree
But no one is there to hear
The bird sings a lament
But not a soul is near.

The brook crackles by
But the plants wither on the banks
The wind whistles and howls
As the soldier from their ranks

The mountains are silent watchers
As uphill the files march
Even the sun shadows over
But there, in the heat, parch

The seas can't hold the tears
Of their near and dear
But they with hearts of steel
Stomp on without fear

The fields see them off
The meadows watch them go
The oblivious men with their heads held high
Prepare to face their foe

The Spirit Of The Past

by Hrishikesh Mokashi

Days of childhood, days of glory,
Days of laughter, nothing to worry.
Days of gold to do or die
Days of dreams to touch the sky!
Buckle up your armour there's a lot to do
The spirit of the past shines within you!

Intelligence and talent divine,
Values that make humanity shine,
Where fraternity has had no fall,
Where unity has bounded and strengthens all!
Let's light this noble fame anew,
The spirit of the past shines within you!

A legacy of Leaders, a glorious past,
*A treasure of gem so brilliant and vast,
A unique blend of new and old,
A future laced with history's gold!
Go join the ranks of priceless few,
The spirit of the past shines within you!

A mischievous smile, a lively grace,
A promising future, a confident face,
Behind it all, a sculptor's hand,
It is possible to make pearls out of dew,
The spirit of the past shines within you!
Conquer the world with every stride
Where the virtue is the loyalty, valour, and pride,
A joy of vibrancy, a unique identity,
An essence that lasts for an eternity!
A salute to that essence so beautiful and true,
The spirit of past shall always shine within you!

Aging Earth

by Hrishikesh Mokashi

Young was the Earth,
And old was the time;
Everything pleasant
Like a wind chime.

All the ancient animals
Along with the trees;
Lived and co-existed
In the harmony and ease.

In this kind of world
Came an obnoxious demon.
Wicked and atrocious,
He was the selfish human.

The animals were horrified,
By this odd, dominant creature;
And he never understood,
That at stake was his future.

The veldts were replaced
By a posh shopping mall,
By the lush green forests
By towers nice and tall.

The ocean became oily,
The blue river grey;
All animals were sick,
The lion was now a prey.

Poor tuskless elephants
Roamed about in vain;
Many helpless animals
Were also brought to pain.

But it is not very long
Humans too are falling,
OH! Listen evil man
The earth is now calling

The Tree

by Hrishikesh Mokashi

A young girl cupped a seed with her palm
And hold on to it secularly
It was a little life after all
For now, it was her responsibility

Finally, once she founded the right spot,
And put the seed into the earth
She waited patiently and eagerly
For mother nature she was giving birth.

She would spend her day in the garden
To see how her plant was growing,
With every little progress she rejoiced
With every little leaf, she was blooming.

Her devotion towards the plant was unconditional
She grew with it as it grew with her,
*She knew that she was all the plant would ever have,
She was its mother, its daughter, its sister.

Time went on and seasons went by,
There was a trunk in place of the stem
The little girl now had also grown old,
Yet everyday she cared for her tree, her treasure, her gem.

When the time came for the old woman,
To leave for her heavenly abode,
She called her little grand daughter
And to her, the beloved tree she showed.

Way Towards Life

by Hrishikesh Mokashi

One smile can start a friendship,
One word can end a fight
One look can end a relationship,
One person can change a life.

Everyday sun gives us sunshine
Then why do we still think about
The old darkness
Let's delete the dark memories
Which pull us back

Life and Time are the best teachers
Life teaches us to make good use of Time
And Time teaches us to have a good Life.

People don't change, they grow up...
The only thing is we should be positive about everything

HEAD UP
STAY STRONG
FAKE A SMILE
MOVE ON

Pretty words are not pretty
If they are not real and true.

In The Journey of Life

by Hrishikesh Mokashi

In the journey of life
Many passers-by's we find
But a real friend is one
Who leaves his imprints behind?

A real friend fills colours
In our world so black and white
He escapes through the dark
And brings in some light

But yet sometimes
We lose the trust in that friend
We misunderstand him
And marks the friendship's end.

But then that,
Friendship is like a precious stone
And its values are known
Only when it's thrown

So don't lose friendship
Coz it is like a rose without thorns
And you will never get it again
Once it is gone.

Miracles

by Hrishikesh Mokashi

Have you ever thought about?
The phenomenon of the setting sun?
How the flowers bloom during
The springtime, one by one?

Ever seen a butterfly
Coming out of its cocoon?
How man has created shuttles
To reach the moon

How a baby learns to speak
His first words, mom, or dad?
How a simple fashion style
Can turn into a school fad

How a baby tadpole can
Turn into a grownup frog
How a venomous snake can
Camouflage into a simple log

How different notes can
Together form a beautiful song
How the roots of a tree
Can be so strong

Everything that is, be it the
Setting of the sun or the
Marking of a new day
All the miracles are
In their own special way.

A Salute to The Great!

by Hrishikesh Mokashi

Your steps have created a path to lead.
Your words have become hymns we heed

Your devotion has led us to success,
Your eyes emit your assuring kindness.

The radiance of your heart and your pure soul
Reaches each one to give them strength to hold.

To hold themselves against the evil,
To hold themselves against the cruel.

Your assertion has made us strong
Your passion has let us come near to what we have longed.

Your promises have been the words of truth
Your love has become remedy for soothe.

The dreams India has are soon going to be a reality
Because you've given our nation its solidity.

You are a boon to this holy *mother land of calm,
We salute you, Oh great Dr. APJ Abdul Kalam*

If Ever Comes Such a Time

by Vedika Pathania

If ever comes such a time
When my hands forget yours,
When the earth halts,
And every word does not resonate the syllables of your name
When sunsets aren't about you and,
I don't trace clouds listening to the songs we wrote,
When I don't whisper poetry to the sky.
If ever comes such a time,
Know that you'll still be mine, in parts.
Like relics, a few memories.
Some yours, some mine.
Way beyond my reach, Way beyond yours.
Tucked in, safely, in the crevices of what we used to be.

A Little While Longer

by Vedika Pathania

Could I get another day with you, maybe?
Or a minute, a moment.
Or perhaps, even a second?
Because time with you, is relative.
If I could have just another day,
I would tell you the same stories and I know you'd listen and
Not tell me that you've heard the same words before.
I would walk with you through the night and I would tell you that I loved you
For one last time.
If I had another minute, I'd hug you as if I were wrapping my arms around your entire existence.
I would breathe in and everything would halt, just for that minute.
I'll find closure in sixty seconds and I'll leave, I promise.
If I had another second, I'd look into your eyes for the longest time because God,

They're the most beautiful ones I've ever seen.
If I had another word, I'll choose it carefully.
If I could just have another moment,

I would find a better way to say goodbye because this time,
I'd know it would be the end.
Just another moment, and I promise I'd let go.

Closest To Closure

by C L Williams

Once upon a time, I thought you were a friend
If only I could see I was ignorant back then
Way back when I could never see the signs
If only then, I could see the truth and realize
When we first met you were nice, you would laugh
A friendship I thought I could never have
It wasn't long after you started acting jaded
What was once genuine, now feels like you're faking
It wasn't soon after you began to act distant
Your once kind words were now feeling less genuine
You said that I said I hated you, not what I said
Said if you picked, me or death, you'd be dead
Fallen to tears, I remember wanting to call
I wanted to apologize, see if this was all my fault
I wanted to know the right words to say
Only want a friend, I think you want me to go away
This time, I'll give in and give you want you want
I'll leave you be, friendship is over, I am done
If I could have one final wish
I wish I knew what I did to deserve this.

The Path of Life

by Aastha Khera

A lonely stride
The walk of life
How long will you walk this side of the knife?
With so much to say
But nothing pours out
Oh where do you hide this mountain of self-doubt
I hear you cry
I hear you laugh
You seldom do, with all your heart
The reflection stares back
And glares beneath
As if it knows way more than me
Because its seen me weep and weep and weep.

Around the hall
You walk tongue-tied
With anxiety in every bite
You sway from one end of the swing to another
Reaching higher every time

But where's the feeling of freedom you felt as a child
Now it's just broken pieces piercing through the heart
Tearing it apart
All the way through the night.
It's like a vacuum pulling you into nothingness for the cost of everything

You laugh in catastrophe
While your mind cries
Cries for help
For care
For love and some pain
And just like that,
You don't laugh anymore
And just like that
Silences are comforting and not daunting
They are now a familiar space
A space you back to
Every now and then
To reach within.

Hours Of Woe

by Sreekala Ajay

The pen moved on the paper,
Cascading the desolation and despair.
Questioning self, is it a failure in decipher,
When did I make my word play unfair?

Letters, 26, might have come out unwittingly,
Liberty of talk, must have come inadvertently,
Now that, my heart cries incessantly,
Expecting the riposte, gently.

May I?
Ask a sorry, for the misspelt words,
May I?
Kneel down before you to get my plea acknowledged.
May I?
Sob whole day long,
May I?
Bend my head on the defeat.

Sorrowful heart, holding back,
Thoughts juvenile of heart so fragile.
Answers sought,
A signature response.

If And But

by Sujatha Menon

Resounding inside out
A forfeit of dreams
Things though untold
Spoke aloud did gestures
Paints of vivid memories
Of a thousand hued folds
Where to it treads
An array of " If's "
Where I know not
But sure into "buts "
Uncertain you are
Through me certain.

How Fortunate, Mon Amour

by Gunjan Makhijani

I'm so lucky,
to be loved by you.
The days that we spent together,
when we promised to be for each other,
were the days when we decided, it has to be forever.
I'm so lucky, to be loved by you.
I don't care if a song like this exists,
'cause all I care about is to be with you, in a mist.
I'm so lucky,
to be loved by you.
They say it's not how it works,
well, when I asked them "how?", their reply had nothing but "perks"!
Why do I have to judge their way of weighing options...
when I crave to meet you,
by being invisibly visible, perhaps with a magical concoction?
Who are they to say it's you who won?
When I know you are the one...
I'm so lucky, to be loved by you.

Moonlight

by Jeysanaah Ganesh

I look up to the night sky
The delicate moonlight shining beyond the scene
Illuminating the seas with a ghastly silver yet majestic green
Clouds blanketed with their sterling lining
Somewhere, someplace
It comforts my heart
Knowing that you're gazing upon the same moonlight
Maybe now, maybe later
Seemingly caught in an endless journey of time differences
And as the world continues to be in slumber
I, in awe of the dazzling sphere of the night sky
Whisper a prayer across to you
Transient in time
As you look up to the same moonlight.

I Wish Someone Taught Me How to Fight

by Siya Kohli

Run, run, run
As far away as you can,
Far enough,
To leave your demons behind.
Far enough
For your darkness to not succumb you,
Far enough
From all the blues,
Run!
As far as you can
To the lakes,
To the woods,
Continue running-
Even if you are running on broken cobblestones,
Twisting your foot with every step,
Trying your best to do it with grace,

Thinking of all the mess you made
As you run in your heels-
Running to chase peace,
Running to chase warmth,
To chase love,
Seek contentment,
Joy,
Pleasure,
Far away from all your anxieties
That surround you,
That put you down
Every time you dream to look up.

I teach you to run
Because they taught me to run
Whenever I felt my blues,
Whenever I saw my demons,
I ran-
As far as I could
To the lakes,
Deep into the woods
To seek contentment,
Chase joy,
Find love,
And be happy-
Until I realized

That it was all an illusion,
That my demons were in me
And I carried them within me
Everywhere I ran.
Even when I ran on broken cobblestones
Twisting my foot
As I ran in my heels,
Trying my best to do it with grace,
Thinking of all the mess I made,
Wishing someone taught me
How to fight
And not to run.

Lessons From a Scarlet Woman

by Siddhi Menon

Built on destitute streets, guilty sheets,
Lies a fortress of life, truth, and hourly lessons,
I pawn my time, bed her stories,
As she teaches me the way of honesty.

A devout pilgrim, comes to her door
He chants, he sings, he preaches divinity,
"He shuns my brothel, he spits on my world
He forgets, it's his God who made me. "

Blue collar ties, selling lies,
The girls and me sell an honest time,
In exchange for a life, a window to the world,
Aren't you too selling your soul in return?

We love, we comfort, we give what's ours,
You city folks, hide behind tints in cars.
I'm a therapist by the hour, lover on call,
I live a life that's truer than you all.

A Gravedigger's Account

by Siddhi Menon

Not in temples or churches,
I found faith in the cemetery.
When a gravedigger walked up to me,
And taught me what life should be.

No riches, no gold, no chariots uphold,
Corpses take to bed, nakedness instead.
Your ego, your pride, are preys for life
A soul's only known, by engravings on a tombstone.

These hands are made for mud,
These eyes are made for despair.
Yet I know life's worth a dime,
And death's already made it's bed.

So I drink to new entrants,
In this nursery for souls,
For death is life indeed,
In a realm that's still unknown.

From The Eyes of a Teenager

by Ananya Purba Sengupta

Little did she know that she is stepping into the most crucial phase of her life where nobody will cajole her to finish things on time, they will just berate her for not finishing it.

What she only knew was her brain and mind were surrounded with a series of questions and they always forced her with new ideas and queries.
She struggled with her ephemeral mood swings which bothered her to the core; all the pleasant sounds were cacophonous to her ears. She wanted someone to alleviate her pain.

Little did she know that all her vicarious feelings are normal for now?
She liked him and had a surge of positive emotion but had to keep it concealed from everyone
around her, she wanted to discuss her fascinating thoughts but with whom?

Little did she know that physical changes are a part of this phase where there should be at least a modicum of excitement, she was more concerned about the newly developed acne on her face.

Little did she know that the fear of exams and the stress for marks are fugacious?
She wanted to share her interest and passion persuasively but felt it was inarticulate for people around her.

Little did she know that being curious about sexual intercourse has nothing to do with her character
she had to choose her words so carefully just to know a little more.
Little did she know that her clandestine activities are just some simple desires of every teenager.

To all the sleepless nights of overthinking, every curious thought that popped in her mind-
To all her struggle to unjumble her feelings -
Every attempt to tolerate the garrulous person around her-
And every stereotypical advice that she tolerated

Before she could realize the emotional rollercoaster or turmoil in her mind, she had missed a lot from this beautiful phase. Before she could define herself or control her emotional differentiation she was into depression.

The Autumn of My Life

by Rachna Goyal

Oh, the wondrous, glorious spring,
Hope eternal ,it does bring,
A new life, new beginning,
Why art thou so fleeting.

The leaves are turning russet and gold,
It's an enchanting sight to behold.
The day so beautiful at dusk,
Enveloping me in its musk.

Take a moment to enjoy,
Pause, ponder and reflect,
Do not wait till the journey's end,
Lest you end up with regret.

The skies with turn dull, dark and grey,
The days chilly, dreary and wet,
Winter will arrive someday,
Death will come, just not yet.

Fallen Out Of Love!

by Vishakha Naware

Early morning the dew settles down on the leaves
Just like the tears roll down my eyes
The dew adorns the green leaves
Just like tears do my cheerless face
I walk in the garden to get some fresh air
Wipe out the tears on my face
Just when the sun comes and washes the dew away
I watch, astonished
In the evening the cricket's noise fills the air
Just like the noise of your memories
Some soothing but mostly infuriating
That shattered the glass of my dreams
I go down the garden to find
That the noise has faded in the dimness of the dawn
Just like your presence in my life
From a gentle dawn to a serrated dusk
I look at the horizon far away
Where you have gone with the luggage called my dreams
I wait for you to come back...

And suddenly, the sky becomes cloudy...
And it rains and mixes my tears with the raindrops
I struggle to separate them from each other
And find out, it is difficult to separate you
From all my memories....
And yet I've finally fallen out of love!

Trapped

by Vishakha Naware

In the chains of my own doing
Trapped
Under the norms of the society
Trapped
Under the expectations of loved ones
Trapped
And getting crushed under the unfathomable heaviness of existence
I see
Colours, a beam of light, a ray of hope.
I realise
I can't change the things around me, so I change the things inside me
Trapped no more
I breathe free.
I breathe the fresh air of realization
Of new beginnings and old endings.

Satisfaction To Be Satisfied

by Vaishnavi Rajput

I smiled and answered,
They heard and befuddled....

They asked "When Will You be Gratified?"
I replied- "When My Satisfaction will be Satisfied."

I explained.......
In this Paradise,
Where some are Clever but some still Wise....
Some are arrogant still some kind
And this is the thing you have to keep in your mind......

Always try to do better than Yesterday,
And you too will agree to my answer someday....

They asked "when will you be Gratified?"
I replied- "When My Satisfaction will be Satisfied."

Thoughts Of a Selenophile

by Soumya Tewari

There were stories I needed to tell,
And had nobody to listen.
So I looked out of the window straight at the moon.
Above me the moonlight glistened.
I had mystical tales to recite,
And few momentarily heartbreaks too.
Each day when I opened the door of my mind,
The moon looked rather anew.
Sometimes full of sparkle,
Sometimes dark as my sorrows,
Sometimes a little bit crescent,
And sometimes a bit narrow.
Day by day, year by year,
I had a connection so strong.
It was like it chased me wherever I went.
Made me feel like everywhere I belonged.
Because I had a friend who illuminated my path
even when the light was gone.
The moon even in its halves,

Never made me feel alone.
So if you ask me
why I love it,
Here's what I want to say -
It's because it gives me hope,
a reason to dream every day.
And shows me that things could be complete even if they're flawed!
And that sometimes solitude in itself is the greatest
reward.

Unconcealed

by Swathi Umashankar

Words would not come out when I opened my mouth.
Though I longed to speak with you, I never could do.
And so the silence grew fuelled by you and by me too.
So much time passed but I knew it could not last.
So why was I not able say something even then?
Fear, an all-consuming fear was the culprit.
My mind telling me I am not worthy anymore.
Never to be seen, nor touched nor thought of at all.
For now, and forever more.
I stand here, at the cusp of parenthood.
Wanting to speak to you once more, tell you about my journey and how I met her.
She loves your stories and lord knows I have more than enough.
Alas it does not near compensate for your presence.
It burns me up knowing I can never be heard by you.
Having given up your physical form, you have moved on.
I desire day I will be able to do so as well.
May you continue to shower your kind blessings on us.

Perception

by Abhav Gupta

The days were bright,
the greenery was a delight
but now it's just dull
and the greenery is another distraction
for the infinitely the seeing eye
I never could see the sun with an open eye
yet I knew how it
looked every day, but now I try to see the sun
and it's just darkness
whether I open or close my eye
12 noon was a time with sun overhead
with no shadow on me but
It feels I am the shadow
with the burden of expectation on me
I used to wait for the sun to set
The moon to rise so that I could
see those which couldn't shine
when it was too bright, but now I wait
for the night just for the darkness

that comes along with it so I can
blend in with something that sees me
The birds could understand me
I could understand them,
Their music was different than any human had then
but now it's just noise,
continuously ringing in my ear
I feel like they are shouting and that's when I cry
People used to be friends and family back then
but now it's just faceless bodies
telling me I couldn't do it yet again
Was it me who was different?
is it me who has changed?
the way I look at things now
is the way everybody looked at me then
I say not that I have not changed but trying to do something you are
Not meant to do does not count here
as if the person wants to change
That is not the world I was used to when I was young, age would change so much is not what I heard.

The New You*

by Sneha Sabu

I wandered through the oval,
In search of acceptance.
It was not the place to look
For what I wanted.
Yet I wanted to be sure,
That I don't miss a chance.
It is the day of global citizens,
Gadgets, BOTS and Artificial intelligence.
Robots replaced humans,
And machines learned to decode
The human mind.
I am not sure
What would give me,
The acceptance of being human.
Botox could give me the looks

The technology the advantage
The training that sharpens my thinking.
But when I get there, I am not indispensable.
There are a thousand others.
Ahead of me or with me
I am not alone,
In this strive for acceptance
For the uniqueness of the self
Is a cliché.
The neo-colonialism has evolved.
It is the era of technological dominance,
Nuclear, bio wars and corporate mafias
The noise of emptiness
Is louder than the deep under currents
Your struggle to belong evolves daily.
And evolution is the new route,
To survival and acceptance.

The Days of Revival

by Sneha Sabu

The smoke of the fire just died
We lost our preserved wildlife!
Our homes in the bushes and
Families just survived.
In months,
The hustle and bustle were over
We were locked up in the four walls.
My tummy kept growing and growing,
I was not pregnant
But worked hours and hours,
In fear of losing my job.
Thanks to the hours,
My shoulder was aching
And slowly it came to my hands
The nerves were tinkling
But I could not stop
For I had tummies to feed
And loans to pay.

I saw my friends fall,
There was no place for bodies anymore.
The cemeteries were filling up,
The hospital beds were full
The human bodies had no home.
There were many wrapped and
Laid on the streets.
Days and months passed,
Some of us lasted
Others left us.
And for those who endured,
It was a battle.
A battle between the virus and livelihood.
The economy collapsed
The gloomy days are soon going to be over.
There is hope amidst hopelessness.
Spring has sprung
The pigeons bred in my balcony
The Indian mynas, the white parrots
Were all happy and chirpy.
If not for the virus
I would have never seen them.
The sky was beautiful,
Every conversation meaningful
And every moment worthwhile.

Life had a new meaning.
If not for the virus
I would not have known,
What a hug and handshake meant,
What a party and social gathering meant.
The social distance broke the wall;
The wall we mended to distance from our fellow.
The struggle for survival united us
The black, brown and white
We're together in this battle
We have forgotten our colours for a change.
The human race is back,
To enjoy the gift of being humane.
The time has come
To cherish small things in life and
Live the life we were meant to live.

The Trial That Changed My Life

by Sneha Sabu

My hands were tied,
I was beaten day and night.
I feel suffocated
Within four walls of the iron bars.

I was arrested last week,
For being at the vicinity of the murder
And for delivering the pizza
To feed my babies.

I am not guilty
Nor have I killed anyone
I was judged unfair
Like the man before me
And is sentenced to death.

I am a migrant
Who has strived for daily bread?
Who worked day and night?
To feed my family.
And here I lie
In the four walls of a cellar
For no fault of mine!
My kids are bullied and mocked at school
For their dad is a murderer.

My wife is out of her job,
For they don't want to hire
A murderer's wife.

I have crossed mountains and waters,
To be in this land
Where I am a stranger.

I have left my father and mother,
For a better morrow
To make a difference in
The lives of my children.

Today all that I worked for is lost
My children need their father,
And my wife, her husband.

I deserve justice.
All I ask for is a fair trial,
To live a fair life.

Eternal Existence

by Ananya Mishra

They say live everyday as if it were your last
Yet somehow the monotonous existence fools you
Into believing that the cruel claws of death, you've surpassed

You try adjusting into your perfect, eternal reality
But you can't, for without the monster of fear
Your life becomes devoid of all purpose and actuality

You strive to locate that thrill in all the flawed places
Now, the countless days start to suffocate you
Hallucinations of Death's façade appear on familiar faces

You soak in every bit of this dreadful feeling
In the hopes that the terror and panic you release
Is enough to lure the ravenous demon

You see it then, lurking behind the narrow shaft
You aren't afraid when you go up to embrace it
For, you had lived that day as if it were your last.

Asthma Attack

by Ananya Mishra

Maybe it was the chilly air I exposed myself to
when I let the wind embrace me, caress me;
or maybe it was because I danced too much-
it was the adrenaline, I swear, not me

Maybe it was the unprovoked laughter or tears-
silly me, should have put my emotions to check;
or maybe the tangy lemonade I treated myself to
turned out to be the most fatal wreck

Whatever it may be, it attacked shamelessly
I battled through coughs but it wasn't enough,
it burnt my lungs and choked my throat-
forced me to sense death's menacing touch

My eyes saw not what was, but what had been;
my mouth whispering, imploring in a silent prayer
as they helplessly watched me getting murdered-
dreading not my blood, but my breath on their hands

No one told me how costly that happy moment was;
heck, I'd die a thousand times over for that smile
but today my doom would not be this predictable
because I survived this before and again I'll survive.

What I Don't Tell You

by Rajlakshmi Kurup

I miss you but I let you go
I love you but I set you free
You are a piece of my heart
The flutter in my womb
The realisation of my dreams
Still I won't beg you to stay
I don't wish to smother
Be a hurdle or block
Or tie strings around your little feet
I will let you fly, reach the skies
For I know if my love is tried and true,
You will seek me one day
Till then, I will wait, at my door or inside my tomb
Know that your footstep will move my womb again,
And I will rest in peace forever!!

Baba

by Tanushree Keshan

Beloved baba,
There are a lot of things I want to say,
I just wish, I could get just one more day.
Every night, before I cry myself to sleep, I sit and pray,
Hoping you can hear me say.

Deep down inside, I know it's by far the best, up there,
But we are not together, which makes it unfair.
You were a gold baba, solid gold,
You not being here, makes everything cold.

You were the reason, family reunion on Diwali was the most ideal,
"Take no. 37, and then you are going win the lottery," I'll miss those deals.
Baba, you were, are and will always be the most loved,
For all of us, you always acted as a cove.

I know you are watching over us, and smiling, even crying a little,
We are not together, and it makes our heart brittle.
At heart, I know you are always here and you still love us with all your heart,
'Cause we share a bond so strong, which can never break apart.

The Yellow Tree

by Prasann Sharma

She sat under a yellow tree
With water droplets still falling on her head
Which were left barely hanging to the leaves after the rain

The sun just diving into the horizon
Painting the sky red
Crickets rubbing their palms and making the
melody of the evening
The curtain of the world cleared by the unexpected
downpour of rain

An evening as cold as to hear the noise of dew still falling on the
surface of the lake miles away
She sat under the yellow tree

In the blankness of the world
Her mind was filled with all the thundering noises inside her head
Her skin looked fine but she was cute deeper in the soul
Heartbroken to the core
She never knew that her screams will ever change
into something different
She never thought that this could happen with her

Yet here he was, standing with her
Only his hands reached her amidst this crowded world,
still for her it was enough to last a lifetime
All the never-ending talks and the never-ending walks

Dark clouds still follow her yet he is there to protect her,
her Knight in the shining armour.
She looked at him and could see her reflection in his eyes,
smiling and proud to have her

All these feelings felt like sunshine to her on a cloudy day encoring
and echoing the very core of her soul

The usher of a new love
The yellow tree stood there
Seeing her all the way through falling in love again

He remembered the good old days when he used to have green
leaves and give shade to anyone and everyone
He remembered how he used to long for the sun on the summer
days trying to hold on to the sun and keep it for himself
But the sun never belonged to him, it was never his, to begin with

It took his love and turned his leaves yellow till the autumn came

But now he sees the girl and how she bloomed
in the new-found love
He knows the autumn has just set in and the winter is long,
still he waits for the sun to rise again.

He knows that his leaves will wither and even the yellow leaves
will leave his side, yet he waits

For the spring to come and his leaves to turn green again and
flutter on the sunny days, for him to gleam again in the sun

Waiting for the spring

The yellow tree stood there
The yellow tree stood there

The Waves

by Divya Naveen

Playing were we, on the sea shore sand
Building house with our own tiny hands

Saving it from the sea that roared
Sending WAVES to the house, it bared

It was what, WAVES, we all meant
When we went to school to emend

Tingling with our hair that grew
Tangling it to make it look brewed

Straight, Wavy, Curly were it called
Mending WAV(Y)ES to the hair, it rolled

It was what, WAVES, we all meant
When we went to college to blend

Analysing what the needs are of business
Working Agile to provide value to business

Sprints, DHs, Burn down charts and PPs
Released in Waves, what we called MVPs

It was what, WAVES, we all meant
When we went to work for money to spend

Sales and profits were on high to start with
2020 we thought would bring in lots of benefits

March did come, lockdown followed
Covid – 19 was what really bellowed

Came in as Waves, first being subtle
Second came in, with people rattled

Vaccines in place, two doses per head
Time it takes, to have all heads covered

It is what, WAVES, we all mean
When we get into 2021 - this year to pertain.

When You Are, I Want to Be

by Ramaponni P

When you are the sun, I want to be the sunshine.
When you are a moon, I want to be a star.
When you are a sky, I want to be a cloud.
When you are a body, I want to be a soul.

When you smile, I want to be that cute dimple.
When you laugh, I want to be a reason for your happiness.
When you cry, I want to be the first one to catch the first drop and wipe the remaining.

When you are sad, I want to be a shoulder to lean on.
When you are serious, I want to be funny.
When you are mature, I want to be childish.
When you are angry, I want to soothe you.

When you walk, I want to hold your hands and feel the warmth.
When you spend your time, I want to earn your attention.
When you respect my feelings, I want to earn your trust.
When you care, I want to shower my affection for you.
When you love me, I want to love you more and more.

Freebird

by Anush Goel

"I'm on my way," he said.
She asked something.
"At the edge of the mountain," he replied.
Eyes brimming with tears,
And mind tangled
in a single thought –
If he could fly, fly so high,
And conquer this gigantic world
Shine so bright, where the world would take him for the sun
Where he would share the serene view with birds
See places untouched by footprints
Away from society
Take control over the loneliness which ensues
Forget the past and move on in life, find the one who can understand him,
And seek his meaningful purpose in life.
It's not easy to get what you want,
And these wishes ungranted were another challenge,

A challenge he was tired of facing alone.

He needed someone who could understand him

Crashing into the right person is a myth, they say.

We all attract what we don't need,

Maybe he attracted her the same way, which makes him want to leave her.

"Hey, are you there?" Whispered she.

"I've arrived at my destination. I'll see you in another life," he said, his voice breaking. Closing his eyes, he flew off the cliff.

Drowning Hard

by Vandana Sudheesh

An illness inclined to our head rather than heart
Being dragged by the hands of fiends
To the fury of loneliness and hatred
A face a sound they abstain from caring
Crowned them by the society of guilelessness
Stress injects the fear at your own behest
Out of control they deny the strength
Unwanted wrappings they open with eagerness
Someone casting spell to own you
In their hands you are bind forever
with no return to your life

Like A Burpee

by Vandana Sudheesh

I wish I could dance with you
In your arms I lay with an enchanting light
Because of you I delayed my fringes of past memories that hurts
A sempiternal brushwork I was made off with love
Your eyes captured my thirst of acquaintance with you
Like in a merry go round I kept swirling into the clouds
My laughs heard like a blasting music from my heart
Living my life at the moment to uncurl the deadliest world
I could see the phosphenes of thankfulness fluttering
My heart in the cushion of your painted words endlessly flawless

Co-Author Biography

Abhav Gupta

Abhav Gupta was born in 2003 in a small town in Punjab called Nabha. Growing up, he was fascinated by the depth of story and poem writing ability and he liked playing badminton too. He first started scribbling poems when he was in class10th and now he is a class 12th pass out and eagerly waiting for his college life that lies ahead. In his free time, he binge-watches shows which often gives him ideas to write about things and his personal favourite show is Riverdale. PERCEPTION is Abhav's first poem to get published.

Hrishikesh Mokashi

Hrishikesh Mokashi is a student of 2nd year Bachelor of Commerce Studying from Savitribai Phule Pune University of Maharashtra. He is a former cricketer and has played for different teams. Also, an avid reader, poet, and blogger, he loves to read fictional, mysterious and autobiographies of famous personalities. He started authoring short stories and poetry from 7th grade itself. He admires and loves the work of famous authors such as O'Henry, Leo Tolstoy, William Shakespeare, R. L. Stevenson, Alfred Lord Tennyson, P. G. Wodehouse and many more. He loves to share his feelings with others, so he writes whenever he feels like it. Till now, he has written more than 21 short stories and 30 poems. A fitness enthusiast, a blogger having love for writing and listening to music, his works are fictional and semi-fictional, hence easily relatable to anyone.

Ananya Mishra

Ananya Mishra is a seventeen-year-old girl trying to figure out life as it comes. For the greater part of her life (mind you, this child is only seventeen), she believed that people would understand her unspoken words and communicate with her silence. When the world did not know how to, she did not unlearn but taught the world instead. Ananya is fluent in art and poetry and has a world that listens. She gave birth to her book "Unfiltered Reality;" has proudly been a part of the 'Covid Diaries' anthology and loves to contribute her work to 'Reflections' magazine. Her creations are honest and raw because what is life if not authentic. "For a million unspoken words inside of me, keep the ones I speak buried respectfully."

Jeysanaah Ganesh

Hailing from Penang, Malaysia, she is an ambivert and a voracious reader, who found writing to be her escape when the voices became a little too loud in her head. Her spilled ink became a vessel for the nuances of her thoughts of melancholy and euphoria. As a person, she believes that everything happens for a reason, and it will eventually fall into place with a minor change in perspective. An engineer by day and dreamer by night, she is a pluviophile, who believes she can take on the world, one cup of coffee at a time.

Aastha Khera

Aastha is just embarking on her journey as a writer and is more excited than ever. You are most likely to find her scribbling in her diary at 3 am next to a tub of ice cream or adoring the moon with all her heart. She derives her love for poetry from the works of Faiz Ahmed Faiz and Juan Elia and is a huge fan of Virginia Woolf. As a first-year student, she is more than thrilled to climb up the ladder as a writer.

Ananya Purba Sengupta

Ananya is an IT engineer by profession and a creative thinker by heart. She loves reading, writing exploring creative stuff. She started writing from a noticeably early age and enjoys putting down her thoughts on paper.

Divya Naveen

Divya - an audacious adventure freak, who believes in having fun at whatever she does. She is passionate about adventure sports and is a periodic poet. She loves travelling and dreams to fly a fighter plane. She believes that there is something good in everyone and considers herself to be a gullible person. She is someone who radiates happiness and positivity around her and believes in the fact that "Whatever happens it is for one's own good".

Gunjan Makhijani

Gunjan Makhijani is pursuing her majors in Journalism from the University of Delhi. She has passed high school with a science stream and has always been inclined towards writing and elocution. She loves exploring different academic disciplines. A wandering mind, but an avid writer at heart.

Jagruthi Kommuri

K.Jagruthi an E-commerce graduate, currently working and an MBA student started writing to express her feelings and loves to write to ignite a little hope and faith in the reader. She is a simple girl who finds solace in words and writes to spread love & positivity to the world. She believes kindness goes a long way when communicated through the heart.

Kriti

Kriti is a twenty-one-year-old finance professional. Till the time a story is intriguing to her, the genre does not matter. One such fascinating mythological tale inspired her to write her first story years ago. She lost her touch with writing outweighed by her ambitions but now, coming back to it has made her happier than ever.

Madhurya Kommuri

Madhurya is an aspiring psychologist by profession and a poet by passion. A perfect imperfection, a beautiful mess is what defines her best. Bringing out the stories people bury inside with patience and comforting with soothing poetry is her little way of bringing peace to minds and making the world a better place to live.

Manoj Vaz

Born in the middle-class underbelly of Mumbai, Manoj started his career as a copywriter in Madison Advertising. He soon realized that he was too independent to toe a line and started his own ad agency, Touché Communications in 1991. In 2016, Manoj shut down his running ad agency and started writing. His first book TINSEL was a hard-hitting saga of the city of Mumbai and its fascination with showbiz. Next, he wrote THE MAGIC CHEST SERIES - a series of crime mysteries for teenagers. He then wrote his acclaimed compilation of short stories and poems - KALEIDOSCOPE. Always challenging himself to not repeat a genre, his latest book is a historical drama – QUEENDOM. A best-seller that is under negotiation to be made into a mega web series. His work has also featured in a dozen anthologies and his book of quotes RANDOM MUSINGS is extremely popular on the internet.

Munmun Aidasani

Munmun Aidasani, Chartered Financial Analyst by profession, hails from the city of lakes, Bhopal (India) currently living in Dubai (U. A. E). She loves wearing many hats. She is an avid and versatile writer, an author, and a blogger. A dreamer with a passion to set up her own benchmark in writing.

When she is not writing, she indulges her children, husband, and loved ones with sumptuous food, with a curious mind trying to see art in everything possible and in quest of exploring new horizons.

Her inner wisdom of being empathic and caring towards her loved ones makes her the best human being around.

She loves writing fiction as well as reality-based inspiring articles. She wants to spread her wings in each genre and believes in versatility.

She can be reached at -
Instagram: @munmunaidasani
Facebook Page: Rising-Mom
Email: aidasanimunmun@gmail.com

Miriam Benjamin

Miriam Benjamin, an 18-year-old literature student from Bengaluru, has always been passionate about writing. She writes eloquently and honestly - calling out human foibles and longings in an unfiltered way. Apart from writing, she indulges in singing and reading.

Rachna Goyal

In her other life, Rachna Goyal holds a degree in Computer Science and a master's in business economics and loves crunching numbers. Happily married, and with two grown-up children, she finds time to pursue her passion for writing poetry. Her poems are an expression of her thoughts, feelings, and experiences. Her poems explore myriad emotions and assorted topics like love, friendship, hope, loss, faith, God, and gender discrimination. Her poems are a celebration of life in all its hues. They are also a window to the poet soul.

Prajwal Shukla

Prajwal Shukla is a prolific writing practitioner, enthusiast and has written over 440 short stories, blogs and articles on socio-economic issues and has a multitude of interests. He likes to explore conceptual fiction writing and a variety of topics in non-fiction as well.

Prasann Sharma

Prasann is an agriculture graduate disciplined by the army, a budding author, and a theatre enthusiast. An example of sheer will and optimism, he is passionate about mythology and finding beauty in every pursuit of life. He is a firm believer of Gandhiji's quote, "Strength doesn't come from the physical being but from the indomitable will." which has helped him overcome all the hurdles in his path. Currently pursuing his MBA from IIM-Kolkata (Calcutta), he aspires to share his imagination with his readers. He is the author of "The Seven Tears of God" a fantasy fiction novel that takes you to a land of elf, fairies, demons etc. He is also the co-author of "Kagzi Khayal." He binge-watches movies and series and has a zeal to learn new things and never misses a chance to do so. He binge-watches movies and series and has a zeal to learn new things and never misses a chance to do so. He is a hodophile, a mythological and a fictional geek who never misses an opportunity to pamper his majestic beast (his bike). He is also close to his family and his dog and puts them above everything.

Rajlakshmi Kurup

Rajlakshmi Kurup works as a freelance writer. She loves writing fiction, short stories, and poems but she also dabbles in non-fiction opinion pieces when inspiration beckons. Her writings have been published in several online and print publications. She lives in Navi Mumbai.

Ramaponni P

Ramaponni is a budding writer and a former HR professional. She likes to learn and explore new things. She always believes that "Life is all about setting and breaking our benchmarks and not about competing with anyone else yet we are all part of the race". She loves reading and aspires to pen down her thoughts straight from her heart.

Shreesh Swaraj

Shreesh, an engineering undergraduate who praises the art involved in writing and is trying to bring some of his wild imaginations into reality through words. He loves authoring short poems and appreciates the beauty that simple words can bring when stitched together.

Soumya Tewari

Soumya is a marketing student who often finds her solace in the world of words. She is a published co-author and a passionate poet, scriptwriter, blogger, and content creator who aspires to bring more happiness and positivity to the world through her write-ups. She has also contributed to a Spotify Podcast named ' Happy Talkies '. Hailing from a small town in Uttar Pradesh, she has always been fascinated by the stories of people around her, and so she loves to compile the simple everyday moments of life into quirky and meaningful tales. When not writing, she can be found binge-watching F.R.I.E.N.D.S, listening to Taylor Swift's music on loop, reading books, gardening in her little balcony garden, and exploring unfamiliar places; mostly cafes and bookstores. Currently, she enjoys writing on platforms like Wattpad, WordPress, Your Quote and Instagram as a hobby. You can connect with her on Instagram @poetrusic_sam.

Siddhi Menon

Siddhi Menon befriended characters in books, wrapped herself in warm, cosy stories and found her wand in a pen. She has been in the advertising industry for over 5 years. She has always been fond of writing, so she naturally chose copywriting as her forte after BMM. She grew close to the creative process and in the meantime loved exploring stories with certain darkness to them. Everybody loves talking about comfortable subjects, but she loves writing so that her words can bring discomfort and an impact. She believes that there is no point of light when there is no darkness to power it.

Siya Kohli

Siya Kohli is a sixteen-year-old who writes poetry for pleasure and believes that extraordinary things do not happen until they do. Poetry, to her, is something incredibly special and personal as it helps her to express her feelings, and well, lighten the weight off her chest! Apart from writing poetry, she loves sitting by the window and reading her book with a cup of hot coffee. She runs a voluntary youth organization on Instagram called K.I.N.D.S. which aims to spread kindness through volunteerism to create a happy and sustainable society. She is also a huge Potterhead and a mad Bollywood fan at heart.

Sneha Sabu

Sneha Sabu is an international strategist, development thinker, motivational speaker and author who has worked for 18 countries in the Asia Pacific region. Sneha has published 25 short stories, 20 poems and several articles on social issues. Sneha is the recipient of Bharath Gaurav Puraskar 2021 and the International Achievers Award 2021. Sneha is a writer of freestyle poetry and is passionate about contemporary and abstract concepts, emotional and humane elements, social and environmental issues. She currently lives and works in Australia.

Sreekala Ajay

Sreekala P. Vijayan is a prolific poet and active member and moderator of Motivational Strips, the World's most active writers' forum. She believes that consistent interactions keeping aside geographic borders, help a poet to be experimental with life lessons. Sreekala's many poems are published in international anthologies and literary magazines. She hails from Palakkad, Kerala, the southern part of India. She is an academician by profession and has groomed many talents among her students. Her poems are apt for an intimate reading and relatable to the common human values seen around. They resonate with amusement, wisdom, and precision. Her ink preference surrounds the varied aspects of poetic art such as environment, nature, pleasure, love, hope, memories, uprising, and many more. Awards received: Ceasar Vallejo 2020 from Union Hispanomundial de escritores. Order of Shakespeare award 2021 Self authored book: Soul in Whole.

Swati Pillai

Born in Thiruvananthapuram, Swati has spent most of her life in the bustling city of Mumbai. Having studied outside India and worked across continents and India, she has experienced the nuances of many cultures. A Corporate Management professional by day, she is also a wife, a mother, a daughter, a dancer, and a singer. She writes whenever she has a calling. With a creative bent of mind, expression comes naturally to her. She makes it a point to give her best in everything she does and has an enjoyable time while doing it.

Sujatha Menon

Sujatha Menon as an upcoming poet is an easy-going, enthusiastic and ambitious woman who is very particular about her career and loves her freedom and respects personal space. She is a postgraduate in English Literature and has completed B.Ed. and qualified N.E.T, S.E.T and other exams. It is her passion to teach and learn new dimensions both in her profession and life. She had a taste in making small verses at an early age but never knew she could really become a poet. Her hobbies are reading, versification, pencil sketching, travelling, and dancing. She loved cooking and is interested in fitness. Right now, she is working in a college as Faculty in the Department of English. She has taken part in an anthology named" The Romantic Breeze" under Upanayan publications.

Swathi Umashankar

Swathi Umashankar is an IT consultant, a job she thought she would not have in a million years! When not clickety-clacking on the laptop, she can be found in the company of her two special men (ahem, cats) Sebastian & Lucifer. She has recently taken up writing again after realizing her love of engaging poems and stories and hopes that it will lead to a kinder and happier world for all. You can reach her at her Insta handle @Pithy_Please and follow her on her Podcast "Pithy Please" and catch up with her on her blog at PithyPlease.com. Pretty please?!!

Vaishnavi Rajput

Life is full of excitement if taken in an optimistic way, one should always relish, venture, explore. Vaishnavi Singh Rajput, currently pursuing law, believes in this. She is a writer by profession and has co-authored many books and has authored a complete book name 'Be Obdurate and Let others make Noise'. She has also got her research paper published in the International Journals of Law. According to her, there shall be one mantra to be followed, 'Pasos Cortos, Vista Larga' which means small steps leads to bigger success. She is bold and a diligent person; she is an extrovert but always prefers to be profoundly serious the time she's working.

Tanushree Keshan

Tanushree Keshan was born on December 9th, 2004, in the north-eastern state of Assam, India. Tanushree loved poetry and fiction from an early age. She is an exceptional student and goes to Budding Buds Senior Secondary School, Tinsukia. For her poetry, Tanushree has been appreciated in her school and various competitions in which she took part. At the mere age of 16, this is her fourth piece of work which has been published. She has been awarded the "Young Writer's Award" and invited to the 'Sahitya Akademi Festival of Letters.' She believes in, "if you can dream it, you can write it."

Vedika Pathania

"Your tale sir, would cure deafness."

Shakespeare believed so, and so does Vedika Pathania, a 19-year-old undergraduate student who believes in the power of words and poetry ever over everything else. Through the years, she has learnt to find refuge in words, art and literature and the simple things in life that make us human. When she is not writing, or struggling to write, you will find her stargazing and staring at the moon or binge-watching every show that exists, there is nothing in between. She hopes that along with warmth, you find parts of yourself and pieces of her in her words, in her poetry.

Vishakha Naware

Vishakha Naware is your typical working mom, juggling work and family! Former journalist and a German language trainer by profession, her passion lies in languages, reading, and authoring short stories! A self-proclaimed Master-Chef, she loves experimenting with new recipes. She loves to travel and explore unfamiliar places and cultures. She is a full-time mom to an active primary schooler. And when she is not running after him for finishing his homework, she likes to binge-watch dramas, thrillers and comedies on Netflix and likes to get lost in the world of books.

Sreeja Chaudhuri

Sreeja Chaudhuri is a student of English Literature. She has been part of several anthologies. Writing is her passion. She is authoring poems since her childhood. Her poems are filled with different emotions about life.

C.L. Williams

C.L. Williams is an international best-selling author living in central Virginia. He's written nine poetry books, five novellas, one novel, and a contributor to a multitude of anthologies and magazines. His most recent release, Tales from the Forbidden Forest, is a connection of short stories written as one collective piece.

Anush Goel

Wanderlust in his veins, Anush Goel is a young entrepreneur. Founder of Inkfeathers Publishing at a very young age of 25, his hobbies encompass travelling, riding bikes, reading, and binging war movies. He loves to build structures, be it organisational or social so that they last in the longer run. With immense experience as a graphic designer, Anush strives to achieve newer milestones every day in his life, however small or big they may be!

Acknowledgements

I extend my whole-hearted gratitude to God, the Almighty for fuelling up me with the beliefs of positivity for the success of compiling and editing this wonderful Anthology.

I thank my co-authors who are unique in their own way for their immense support and love towards the anthology and for bringing my dreams to reality.

Special thanks to Utkarsh for hiring me to this amazing platform and giving me a golden chance to accomplish my dream.

I thank Inkfeathers Publishing and the team, especially Tanishk, for all their genuine support granted to me whenever needed.

Last but not least I would thank my mentors, friends, relatives for the untiring support and appreciation they have given me throughout my life.

Vandana Sudheesh

INKFEATHERS PUBLISHING

India's Most Author Friendly Publishing House

Stay updated about the latest books, anthologies, events, exclusive offers, contests, product giveaways and other things that we do to support authors.

Inkfeathers Publishing

@InkfeathersPublishing

@_Inkfeathers

@Inkfeathers

Inkfeathers.com

We'd love to connect with you!